PIERRE-AUGUSTE
RENOIR

PIERRE-AUGUSTE
RENOIR

Nancy Nunhead

BARNES
&NOBLE
BOOKS
NEW YORK

This edition published by
Barnes and Noble Inc.,
by arrangement with Brompton
Books Corporation

Produced by Brompton Books
Corporation
15 Sherwood Place
Greenwich, CT 06830

Copyright © 1993 Brompton Books
Corporation

ISBN 1-56619-179-3

Printed in Spain

Reprinted 1994

PAGE 1: *Portrait of Madame
Chocquet,* 1875

PAGE 2: *The End of the Lunch,*
1879

PAGE 4: *Dancing Girl with
Tambourine,* 1909

CONTENTS AND LIST OF PLATES

INTRODUCTION

The paintings of the Impressionist movement which flourished in France from the late 1860s enjoy an unparalleled popularity among art lovers today, through numerous exhibitions, books, and posters. But perhaps no paintings enjoy a more widespread popularity than those of Pierre-Auguste Renoir. His luscious representations of contented families, shapely bathing beauties, and sun-filled landscapes seem to recreate for the modern viewer a lost paradise.

This lushness which is so appealing is also, however, one of the greater obstacles to reaching an understanding of Renoir's art. For rather than conjuring a vision of some lost nineteenth-century Eden, what these images present us with are evidence of the artist's own attitudes to society and how he felt it should be organized. This complexity is inextricably interwoven with his own life and views about how he progressed from humble origins.

Pierre-Auguste Renoir was born on 25 February 1841 at Limoges in central France, the sixth child of Léonard Renoir and his wife Marguérite Merlet. In 1844 the family moved to Paris where Léonard earned his living as a tailor. In 1854 Auguste left school, aged 13, and went to work as a porcelain decorator for the firm Lévy frères. His precocious gift for this work is recorded and it may help account for Renoir's lifelong respect for craft skills. His equal mistrust for mechanization is probably due to the fact that this was the cause of Lévy frères' bankruptcy in 1858: other manufacturers using mechanical processes could always undercut the price of handpainted work. Out of work, Renoir made a meager living decorating fans and blinds.

In January 1860 Renoir successfully applied for permission to copy paintings in the Louvre, a practice popular among students of fine art and one he was to follow for the next four years. His taste at this time was for rococo works of the eighteenth century such as those by Fragonard, Watteau, Boucher, and Lancret. Boucher's *Bath of Diana* is said to have been a particular favorite of Renoir's. Although he was later to make a number of paintings of bather subjects, at this date it seems to have been the painting's frothily handled paint and light tonality which appealed to Renoir.

Renoir's pursuit of a career as a 'proper' painter began to take shape in 1861 when he enrolled at the Paris studio of Charles Gleyre, a Swiss painter and teacher who offered free tuition and charged only 10 francs a month to cover models' fees. Gleyre's own paintings had achieved a modest amount of success at the Salon, the annual exhibition controled by the Ecole des Beaux-Arts. His works were polished in execution but Romantic in mood and the Salon still preferred classical subjects. Gleyre had as a young man met the

RIGHT: Boucher's *Bath of Diana* was reputed to be one of Renoir's favorite paintings. He admired the subject, one he was to tackle himself on several occasions, the light tonality, and the frothy handling of the paint.

LEFT: Renoir's master Charles Gleyre painted *Evening: Lost Illusions* in 1843. It was a great success at the Salon.

BELOW: Alexandre Cabanel's *Birth of Venus* was admired by Emperor Napoleon III at the 1863 Salon. Female nudes of this type were popular at the Salons, their classical allusions lending them a strong gloss of respectability, even high-mindedness.

English landscape painter Richard Parkes Bonington and this encounter perhaps encouraged Gleyre to practice this genre and to encourage his pupils to do likewise. Renoir clearly liked and respected his master and continued to refer to himself as a 'pupil of Gleyre' long after Gleyre's death in 1874. Two tenets of Gleyre's teaching were to stay with Renoir: the importance of drawing as the basis of painting and the need to work on landscape painting in the open air.

In 1862, while he was still a pupil at Gleyre's, Renoir enrolled for two years at the Ecole des Beaux-Arts in Paris. This clearly reflects Renoir's desire to succeed, as success for any painter was very much dependent at this time on his (or occasionally her) exhibiting at the Salon, a huge annual exhibition whose jury was principally composed of Professors at or members of the Ecole. It is thought Renoir submitted a work to the 1863 jury but if he did it was rejected along with an unprecedentedly large number of other works. The outcry which this wholesale rejection provoked led Emperor Napoleon III to sanction an alternative exhibition for all the unsuccessful artists, the Salon des Refusés. Although many artists chose not to exhibit there because of the fear of stigma at being associated with refusal, the show did provide a model of sorts for other alternative exhibitions such as the Impressionist exhibitions of 1874-86.

RIGHT: Fantin-Latour's *A Studio in the Batignolles* depicts Manet's studio and his admiring circle, which included Renoir, seen here in a hat. Monet is the shadowy figure at the right.

Renoir's first Salon success came in 1864 when he had a painting based on Victor Hugo's enormously popular novel *Notre Dame de Paris* accepted. He seems later to have been dissatisfied with the work and destroyed it. Although Renoir continued to submit to the Salon he never again sent in any such '*grandes machines*', as huge paintings with literary or historical subjects were called. In 1865 he sent in a portrait of William Sisley, father of his friend and painter Alfred Sisley, and such relatively small and informal works typified his Salon submissions henceforth.

Alfred Sisley had been a fellow-pupil of Renoir's at Gleyre's, as had Claude Monet and Frédéric Bazille. Other painters who met at this time were Camille Pissarro and Paul Cézanne, who had attended the Académie Suisse, run on similar lines to Gleyre's. Thus by 1863 the core of the future Impressionist group had met one another. Some of the ideas that were to unite them were explored by Renoir, Bazille, Sisley, and Monet on a painting trip they took to Chailly in the Forest of Fontainebleau during Easter 1863. Although they worked in the open air, in the manner recommended by Gleyre and by Barbizon painters such as Millet and Corot, they did not consider the works they then

LEFT: A cartoon from the *Journal Amusant* of 1869 pokes gentle fun at the amateur artists who followed the example of the Barbizon and future Impressionist painters by working in the open air.

RIGHT: The bathing place called La Grenouillère on the Seine where Monet and Renoir painted together in 1869.

produced as suitable to be exhibited as finished paintings. They merely formed the basis of larger studio-produced works, with figures and other details added, acting as aide-mémoires of such natural and ephemeral effects as sunlight. It was many years before Renoir executed completely in the open air paintings he considered worthy of exhibition.

The increasing practice artists such as Monet and Renoir made of working in the open air was facilitated greatly by advances that had been made in the production of artists' materials. By the 1860s ready-mixed paint in collapsible metal tubes was available, as were light-weight, easily portable sketching easels. Renoir painted Monet using just such an easel in *Claude Monet Painting in his Garden at Argenteuil* (1873; Wadsworth Atheneum, Hartford, Connecticut). Such materials would have been crucial to Monet and Renoir when they worked together in the summer of 1869 painting at La Grenouillère, a bathing and boating establishment on the Seine. Although Monet's letters of the time suggest that these paintings, including Renoir's, were just sketches for larger finished works they both proposed to make later, they did subsequently sign them, usually an indication of the artist's satisfaction that a work had reached a completed state.

Certainly compared to his other early landscapes, Renoir's paintings at La Grenouillère are revolutionary in their use of color, handling of paint, and apparent spontaneity of composition. The choppy brushwork is used to indicate very immediate effects of sunlight

through foliage and across the rippling surface of the river. The palette is notably different from the restricted palette of earth colors he had used for earlier, studio-produced landscapes and is remarkable for the lightness and purity of the colors, an effect achieved by mixing pure color with white, emulating the practice of those eighteenth-century masters he admired. The composition, although no doubt carefully thought out, gives an appearance of spontaneity in the way that elements such as the boats are cut off apparently arbitrarily.

By the early 1870s Renoir was beginning to enjoy some success as a painter. In 1870 he had had a work accepted for the Salon and in 1872 the dealer Paul Durand-Ruel, whom Monet had introduced to Renoir and who was to be an important early promoter of the Impressionists, bought one of his works. But it was perhaps his failure to have a work accepted at the 1873 Salon which prompted Renoir to join a group of other disaffected and likeminded young painters in setting up the first Impressionist exhibition. As in 1863 a Salon des Refusés was held in 1873, but many artists yearned for a truly independent forum in which to exhibit their work. In December 1873 Renoir, Monet, Pissarro, Berthe Morisot, Sisley, and Degas, among others, registered themselves as a joint stock company for the purposes of staging an exhibition of their work. A major impetus for all of them, though especially for Camille Pissarro and Paul Cézanne who had been unremittingly unsuccessful in their submissions to the Salon, was the need to find

new markets for their work. This had become all the more pressing since Paul Durand-Ruel had had to limit his acquisitions, having got himself into financial difficulties.

The exhibition, which ran from 15 April to 15 May 1874 with long opening hours to encourage sales, included seven works by Renoir, including *La Loge* (1874; Courtauld Institute Galleries, London). It was held in a studio in the boulevard des Capucines formerly occupied by the photographer Nadar, and the flock wallpaper and mixture of natural and gaslight was thought to approximate conditions under which works would be seen in the average household. A major departure from the way works were displayed in the Salon was that the exhibits were hung mostly on one level so that none was displayed too disadvantageously. Despite frequent references to the failure of the exhibition it was visited by 3500 people during the month it was open. One critic, Louis Leroy, famously used the term 'impressionist' derogatively in describing a version of Monet's *Impression, Sunrise*, but many other critics found something positive to say about the works on display.

Despite the number of visitors business was not brisk

and at the close of the exhibition each exhibitor was left owing 185 francs 50 centimes. To help clear their debts and to generate more publicity Monet, Renoir, Morisot, and Sisley held an auction of their work in March 1875. Renoir sold 20 paintings for a total of 2251 francs, but some fetched as little as 50 francs. He did succeed, however, in securing two new commissions. One was from Victor Chocquet, a civil servant and early enthusiast for the Impressionists, for a portrait of his wife Caroline. The other was from industrialist Jean Dollfuss who wanted Renoir to paint a copy of Delacroix's *Jewish Wedding*, a painting in the Louvre. Renoir's copy reveals the extent to which he could adapt his style when economic pressures obliged him to. By the time of the second Impressionist exhibition in 1876, nine of Renoir's exhibited works had already been sold so were listed as loans. Although exhibiting works as 'already sold' was a device used by several of the Impressionists to stimulate desire for their work, it does suggest that Renoir had begun to find a market for his work.

Perhaps heartened by these successes, in the summer of 1876 Renoir began a large-scale work. Its subject was the Moulin de la Galette, a dance hall in Montmartre, an area of Paris which still retained a rustic atmosphere in

FAR LEFT: Monet painted *Bathers at La Grenouillère* alongside Renoir in 1869.

LEFT: The former studio of the photographer Nadar on the boulevard des Capucines was the location for the first Impressionist exhibition in 1874.

RIGHT: The Moulin de la Galette in Montmartre was a popular haunt for Renoir and many of his associates, and featured in numerous paintings. Montmartre still retained something of its rustic atmosphere at this time.

the 1870s. Renoir probably worked on a sketch or sketches in the open air and produced the large-scale version in his studio. Nonetheless he succeeds in investing it with many of the qualities of high tone and fleeting light effects he had captured in his on-the-spot studies. The painting *The Ball at the Moulin de la Galette*, showed many of his friends sitting and dancing in the Moulin's garden and it was exhibited at the third Impressionist exhibition in 1877. During the exhibition a journal, *L'Impressioniste*, was produced, mainly written by Renoir's future biographer, Georges Rivière. He wrote approvingly of the *Ball at the Moulin de la Galette*:

Certainly M Renoir has a right to be proud of his *Ball* . . . It is a page of history, a precious moment of Parisian life depicted with rigorous exactitude. Nobody before had thought of capturing some aspect of daily life in a canvas of such large dimensions . . . He has attempted to produce a contemporary note and he has found it.

What Renoir had done was to realize an ambition of many writers and painters of the realist and naturalist traditions, by creating a work which captured the particularities of contemporary life and presented them on a scale usually reserved for historical, allegorical, or literary subjects.

The late 1870s saw the official recognition afforded Renoir's work reach a much greater level. He had works accepted at the Salons of both 1879 and 1880. A law prevented exhibitors at the Impressionist shows from exhibiting at the Salon and in both 1878 and 1881 Renoir chose to exhibit at the Salon rather than at the fourth and fifth Impressionist shows. Part of his motive was financial, as his fellow Impressionists such as

Pissarro understood. For him to succeed he had to keep exhibiting at the Salon. Nonetheless he offered an alternative excuse to Paul Durand-Ruel for his failure to exhibit at the 1881 Impressionist exhibition:

For me to exhibit with Pissarro, Gauguin, and Guillaumin would be like exhibiting with any socialist . . .

During 1880 Durand Ruel had spent 16,000 francs on Renoir's paintings and Renoir took the opportunity offered by this financial liquidity to travel, first to North Africa, then to Italy. The first trip to Algeria in March and April 1881 confirmed many of his interests of the previous 10 or 15 years. Since French colonization of North Africa the sights and especially the women of North Africa had become popular as emblems of exoticism, as Renoir's *Parisiennes in Algerian Dress* (1872), a work shown at the 1872 Salon, clearly demonstrates. A less superficial and therefore far more significant influence on Renoir's art in the 1880s was his trip to Italy from October 1881 to March 1882.

What Renoir saw in Italy which so moved him were the classical Roman frescoes, some from Pompeii, which he saw in the Museo Nazionale in Naples, and Raphael's decorations of the villa Farnesina in Rome. Renoir's discovery of these works came at a crucial time for him as he was questioning himself about the limitations of impressionism. One of the objectives of the impressionist style had been the accurate analysis and recording of effects of light and color reflexions on objects in the open air. But as Renoir came increasingly to realize, this automatic or objective recording of ephemeral effects was an unattainable goal, as it relied on the artist

LEFT: Paul Durand-Ruel (1832-1923) was the first dealer to buy the works of the Impressionist painters, including Renoir, in significant numbers.

ABOVE RIGHT: A sheet of studies for the *Bathers*, 1887, one of the key works in the characteristic 'dry' style of the 1880s which was often applied to classical subjects.

attempting to translate what were, to start with, his own subjective impressions into paint. The picture surface was in danger of breakdown. What was needed to prevent this was a new approach, based on drawing providing an underlying structure. This approach had been recommended by his master Gleyre and it was exemplified admirably by Raphael and the Roman artists of Pompeii.

A further impetus to Renoir seeking a new and potentially lucrative idiom was increasing family responsibilities. In 1879 he had met Aline Charigot, a young woman from north-eastern France. Although they did not marry until 1890 their first son, Pierre, was born in 1885. But if Renoir's motives for a change of style were in part financial he was not at first successful. His first essays in the new style were *The Children's Afternoon in Wargemont* and the *Bathers*. The composition of the latter was based on a seventeenth-century classicizing bas-relief in the gardens of the Palace of Versailles and remained unsold for some time after it was exhibited in May 1887. The change in Renoir's style is exemplified within one painting, *The Umbrellas*, begun in 1881 but not completed until 1886; while the righthand side is in the older impressionist mode, with soft brushwork and high tonality, the left side is much smoother in finish and more somber in tonality.

But the disapproval former enthusiasts for his

impressionst style felt for the new approach had the happy converse of increasing Salon acceptability. As well as looking for a new sense of structure in his paintings, Renoir was increasingly to concentrate on the female nude, the archetypal classical and therefore favored Salon subject. Renoir's decision to exhibit solely at the Salon was due in part to his suspicions about what had happened to the Impressionist exhibitions. He came increasingly to feel that they were being usurped by artists whose views did not accord (artistically in the case of Gauguin, politically in the case of Pissarro) with his own. Although he could not prevent Durand-Ruel from exhibiting 27 of his works the dealer owned in the 1882 show, Renoir did not exhibit at the eighth and final exhibition of 1886.

The 1880s, as well as seeing a change in his approach to his work, were also years of increasing prosperity for Renoir. This is reflected in the scenes of comfortable bourgeois life, both his own and his patrons', which he increasingly preferred to paint. Renoir has been much criticized for his misogyny and for his reactionary political views. While it is true that many of his statements were anti-Semitic and that he was anti-Dreyfus, his views were not unusual in late nineteenth-century France and he did cultivate and socialize with his Jewish patrons. His attitude toward women is more complex and difficult. Although he respected and greatly admired the work of Berthe Morisot, he professed much

LEFT: A Renoir sketch of the painter Berthe Morisot and her daughter Julie Manet, who became Renoir's ward in 1895 following her mother's death.

to prefer women who were uneducated and confined to rearing children. This view is consistent with his broader belief in the merits of a hierarchical society with everyone knowing their correct place within the pecking order. His views are certainly reflected in the way he presents women in his paintings, either as objects (of beauty or sexual desirability) or in the conventional domestic roles.

From the 1890s until his death in 1919 Renoir certainly had a ready supply of subjects for his domestic scenes. The birth of his first son Pierre had been followed in 1894 by Jean, later celebrated as a film director, and in 1901 by Claude, known as Coco. In 1896 a cousin of Mme Renoir, Gabrielle Renaud, joined the household to help with the children. Renoir painted her many times, on her own or with one or more of his sons. The last twenty years of Renoir's life were plagued with ill health

and disability. From his fifties he had suffered from arthritis and this had been compounded by rheumatism and the partial atrophy of a nerve in his left eye.

Renoir's final years were, despite these trials, highly prosperous. His work was skilfully promoted by the dealer Ambroise Vollard whom he had first met in the 1890s. Vollard went on to become one of the most successful dealers in the first half of the twentieth century. He owed his success to his ability to spot greatness in the making. It was Vollard who in 1913 suggested to Renoir that he branch out into sculpture which was, in his seventies, a new art for him. Vollard introduced him to the young sculptor Richard Guino (1890-1973) who was to act as his hands. Guino successfully interpreted in cast bronze Renoir's favored subjects of nudes and mothers in a way that is both classical and massively monumental.

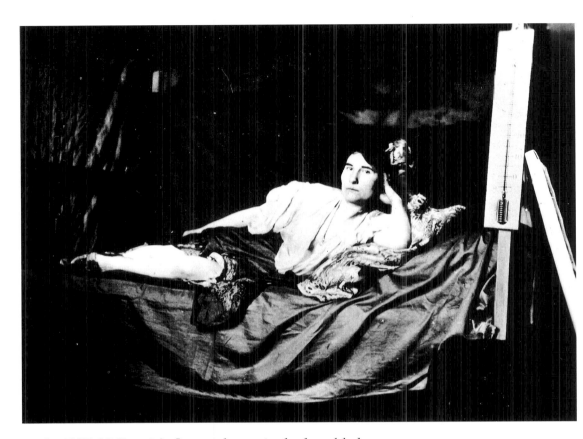

LEFT: Gabrielle Renard, a
cousin of Mme Renoir, joined
the household in 1895 to help
with the children; Renoir
frequently used her as a model,
with or without his children.

In 1907-08 Renoir's financial security had enabled
him to build himself a house and studio at Cagnes in the
south of France, which even in winter has a mild, dry
climate supposedly beneficial to rheumatism. But for the
last few years of his life he was confined to a wheelchair
and had to have his brushes strapped to his hands; this
may account for the rather loose brushwork in his final
paintings. Renoir died at Cagnes, aged 78, on 3
December 1919; only Monet among the other
Impressionist painters outlived him to enjoy even greater
national adulation.

RIGHT: In 1913 the dealer
Ambroise Vollard encouraged
Renoir to produce bronze
sculptures in collaboration with
Richard Guino.

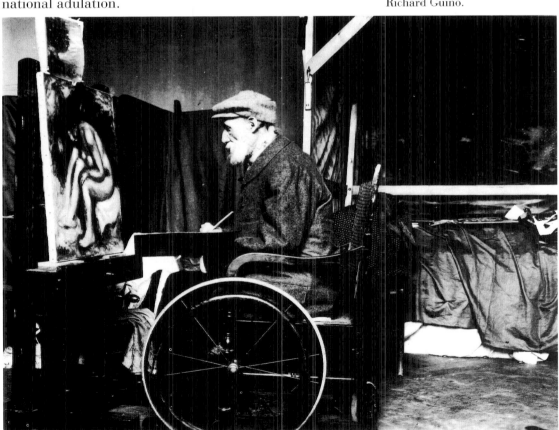

LEFT: In his final years
rheumatism and arthritis
confined Renoir to a wheelchair.

RIGHT:
Bouquet of Spring Flowers
1866, oil on canvas, 39¾×31¹/₁₀ inches (101×79 cm)
Fogg Art Museum, Harvard University, Cambridge,
Massachusetts
Grenville L Winthrop Bequest

ABOVE:
William Sisley
1864, oil on canvas, 32½×25¾ inches (81.5×65.6 cm)
Musée d'Orsay, Paris

ABOVE:
Jules Le Coeur in the Forest of Fontainebleau
1866, oil on canvas, 41¾×31½ inches (106×80 cm)
Museu de Arte de São Paulo

LEFT:
Mother Anthony's Inn at Marlotte
1866, oil on canvas, 76¾×51⅙ inches (195×130 cm)
Nationalmuseum, Stockholm

PAGE 20:
Portrait of Bazille
1867, oil on canvas, 41⅓×27½ inches (105×70 cm)
Musée d'Orsay, Paris

PAGE 21:
Diana
1867, oil on canvas, 78½×51 inches (199.5×51 cm)
National Gallery of Art, Washington
Chester Dale Collection

RIGHT:
The Pont des Arts
1867, oil on canvas, 24½×40½
inches (62.2×102.9 cm)
The Norton Simon Foundation,
Pasadena, California

PAGE 24:
Lise with a Parasol
1867, oil on canvas, 72½×45¼
inches (184×115 cm)
Folkwang Museum, Essen

PAGE 25:
Summer (Lise)
1868, oil on canvas, 35×24½
inches (89×62 cm)
Staatliche Museen Preußischer
Kulturbesitz, Nationalgallerie Berlin

PAGE 26:
Alfred Sisley and his Wife
c. 1868, oil on canvas, 42⅛×30
inches (107×76 cm)
Wallraf-Richartz-Museum, Cologne

PAGE 27:
The Clown
1868, oil on canvas, 76×51⅙
inches (193×130 cm)
Kröller-Müller Museum, Otterlo

Nymph by a Stream
c. 1869, oil on canvas, 26⅜×48¾ inches (67×124 cm)
National Gallery, London

La Grenouillère
1869, oil on canvas, 26×33⅞ inches (66×86 cm)
Nationalmuseum, Stockholm

La Grenouillère
1869, oil on canvas, 25½×36⅝ inches (65×93 cm)
Oskar Reinhart Collection
'Am Römerholz,' Winterthur

ABOVE:
Portrait of Renoir's Father
1869, oil on canvas, 24×18 inches (61×45.7 cm)
The Saint Louis Art Museum, St Louis, Missouri; Museum
Purchase

RIGHT:
Flowers in a Vase
c. 1869, oil on canvas, 25½×21⅜ inches (64.9×54.2 cm)
Museum of Fine Arts, Boston
Bequest of John T Spaulding

Odalisque: Woman of Algiers
1870, oil on canvas, 27¼×48¼ inches (69.2×122.6 cm)
National Gallery of Art, Washington DC
Chester Dale Collection

Bather with a Griffon
1870, oil on canvas, 72½×45¼ inches (184×115 cm)
Museu de Arte de São Paulo

Madame Clémentine Stora (L'Algérienne)
1870, oil on canvas, 33×23⅝ inches (84×60 cm)
Fine Arts Museum of San Francisco
Gift of Mr and Mrs Prentis Cobb Hale in honor of Thomas
Carr Howe, Jr

ABOVE:
Bouquet in a Theater Box
c. 1871, oil on canvas, 15¾×20 inches (40×51 cm)
Musée de l'Orangerie, Paris

RIGHT:
Still Life with Bouquet
1871, oil on canvas, 29½×22⅞ inches (75×58 cm)
Museum of Fine Arts, Houston

A. Lenoir 72

The Pont Neuf
*1872, oil on canvas, 29½×37 inches
(75×94 cm)*
National Gallery of Art, Washington DC
Ailsa Mellon Bruce Collection

LEFT:
Parisiennes in Algerian Dress
1872, oil on canvas, 61¾×51½ inches (157×131 cm)
National Museum of Western Art, Tokyo
Matsukata Collection

ABOVE:
Claude Monet Reading
1872, oil on canvas, 24×19⅝ inches (61×50 cm)
Musée Marmottan, Paris

Monet Painting in his Garden at Argenteuil
1873, oil on canvas, 18³/₈×23¹/₂ inches (47.1×60.1 cm)
Wadsworth Atheneum, Hartford, Connecticut
Bequest of Anne Parrish Titzell

ABOVE:
Riding in the Bois de Boulogne
1873, oil on canvas, 102½×89 inches (261×226 cm)
Kunsthalle, Hamburg

RIGHT:
La Parisienne
1874, oil on canvas
63×41¾ inches (160×106 cm)
National Museum of Wales, Cardiff

LEFT:
Dancer
1874, oil on canvas, 56⅛×37⅛ inches (142.5×94.5 cm)
National Gallery of Art, Washington DC
Widener Collection

La Loge
1874, oil on canvas, 31½×24¾ inches (80×63 cm)
Courtauld Institute Galleries, University of London

The Seine at Argenteuil
1874, oil on canvas, 19⅝×23⅝ inches
(50×60 cm)
Portland Art Museum, Portland, Oregon

Madame Monet and her Son Jean in the Garden at Argenteuil
1874, oil on canvas, 19⅞×26¾ inches (50.4×68 cm)
National Gallery of Art, Washington DC
Ailsa Mellon Bruce Collection

Portrait of Claude Monet
1875, oil on canvas, 33½×23½ inches (85×60 cm)
Musée d'Orsay, Paris

Portrait of Victor Chocquet
1875, oil on canvas, 18⅛×14⅛ inches (46×36 cm)
Oskar Reinhart Collection 'Am Römerholz,' Winterthur

Les Grands Boulevards
1875, oil on canvas, 20½×25 inches (52.1×63.5 cm)
Philadelphia Museum of Art
The Henry P McIlhenny Collection in
memory of Frances P McIlhenny

Copy of Delacroix's 'Jewish Wedding,'
1875, oil on canvas, 43×57 inches (109.2×144.8 cm)
Worcester Art Museum, Worcester, Massachusetts

Snowscape
c. 1875, oil on canvas, 20×26 inches
(51×55 cm)
Musée de l'Orangerie, Paris
Collection Walter et Guillaume

ABOVE:
Portrait of Madame Chocquet
1875, oil on canvas, 29½×23⅝ inches (75×60 cm)
Staatsgalerie, Stuttgart

RIGHT:
The Swing
1876, oil on canvas, 36¼×28¾ inches (92×73 cm)
Musée d'Orsay, Paris

The Ball at the Moulin de la Galette

1876, oil on canvas, 51½×68⅞ inches (131×175 cm)

Musée d'Orsay, Paris

Path through the Long Grass
1876-77, oil on canvas
23¼×28¾ inches (59×73 cm)
Musée d'Orsay, Paris

Madame Charpentier and her Children
1878, oil on canvas
60½×74⅞ inches (153.7×190.2 cm)
Metropolitan Museum of Art, New York
Wolfe Fund, 1907
Catharine Lorillard Wolfe Collection

The Wave
1879, oil on canvas, 25½×39 inches
(64.8×99.2 cm)
The Art Institute of Chicago
Potter Palmer Collection

PAGE 72:
The Café-Concert
1876-77, oil on canvas, 25½×19⅝ inches
(65×50 cm)
National Gallery, London

PAGE 73:
Jugglers at the Cirque Fernando
1879, oil on canvas, 51¾×39⅙ inches
(132.5×100.2 cm)
The Art Institute of Chicago
Potter Palmer Collection

The Skiff
c. 1879, oil on canvas
28×36¼ inches (71×92 cm)
The National Gallery, London

PAGE 76:
The End of the Lunch
1879, oil on canvas
39⅙×32¼ inches (99.5×82 cm)
Städelsches Kunstinstitut, Frankfurt

PAGE 77:
On the Terrace
c. 1879, oil on canvas
39½×39⅞ inches (100.5×81 cm)
The Art Institute of Chicago
Mr and Mrs Lewis Larned
Coburn Collection

Irène Cahen d'Anvers
1879, oil on canvas, 25½×21½ inches (65×54 cm)
E G Bührle Collection, Zurich

Place Clichy
c. 1880, oil on canvas, 25½×21¼ inches (65×54 cm)
Fitzwilliam Museum, Cambridge

The Luncheon of the Boating Party
1881, oil on canvas, 51×68 inches (129.5×172.7 cm)
The Phillips Collection, Washington, DC

LEFT:
Pink and Blue: The Cahen d'Anvers Girls
1881, oil on canvas, 46⅝×29⅛ inches (119×74 cm)
Museu de Arte de São Paulo

ABOVE:
Arab Festival, Algiers
1881, oil on canvas, 28¾×36¼ inches (73×92 cm)
Musée d'Orsay, Paris

Venice: Piazza San Marco
1881, oil on canvas, 25¾×32 inches
(65.4×81.3 cm)
The Minneapolis Institute of Arts
John R Van Derlip Fund

Fruits of the Midi
1881, oil on canvas, 20×25¾ inches (50.7×65.3 cm)
The Art Institute of Chicago
Mr and Mrs Martin A Ryerson Collection

Rocky Crags, l'Estaque
1882, oil on canvas, 26⅛×37⅞ inches (66.5×81 cm)
Museum of Fine Arts, Boston
Julia Cheney Edwards Collection

LEFT:
By the Seashore
1883, oil on canvas, 36¼×28½ inches (92×72.4 cm)
The Metropolitan Museum of Art, New York
Bequest of Mrs H O Havemeyer
The H O Havemeyer Collection, 1929

ABOVE:
Wagner
1882, oil on canvas, 20⅞×18⅛ inches (53×46 cm)
Musée d'Orsay, Paris

Dance at Bougival
1883, oil on canvas
71½×38½ inches
(182×98 cm)
Museum of Fine Arts, Boston
Picture Fund Purchase

Dance in the Country
1883, oil on canvas
70⅞×35½ inches (180×90 cm)
Musée d'Orsay, Paris

LEFT:
Dance in the City
1883, oil on canvas, 70⅞×35½ inches (100×90 cm)
Musée d'Orsay, Paris

ABOVE
Portrait of Aline Charigot
c. 1885, oil on canvas, 25½×21¼ inches (65×54 cm)
Philadelphia Museum of Art

Moulin Huet Bay, Guernsey
1883, oil on canvas, 11½×21¼ inches (29×54 cm)
National Gallery, London

**The Children's Afternoon
at Wargemont**
1884, oil on canvas
51⅙×67 inches (130×170 cm)
Statliche Museen Preußischer
Kulturbesitz, Nationalgalerie, Berlin

La Roche-Guyon
c. 1885, oil on canvas, 18½×22 inches (47×56 cm)
Aberdeen Art Gallery

PAGE 100:
Bathers
1887, oil on canvas, 46⅜×67¼ inches (117.8×170.8 cm)
Philadelphia Museum of Art
Mr and Mrs Caroll S Tyson Collection

LEFT:

The Umbrellas
1881-82 and 1885-86, oil on canvas, 70⅞×45¼ inches
(180×115 cm)
National Gallery, London

ABOVE:

Little Girl with a Sheaf of Corn
1888, oil on canvas, 25½×21¼ inches (65×54 cm)
Museu de Arte de São Paulo

ABOVE:
Montagne Sainte-Victoire
*c. 1888-89, oil on canvas, 20⅞×25¼ inches
(53×64 cm)*
Yale University Art Gallery, New Haven, Connecticut
The Katharine Ordway Collection

RIGHT:
The Apple-Seller
c. 1890, oil on canvas, 26×21¼ inches (66×54 cm)
Cleveland Museum of Art
Bequest of Leonard C Hanna Jr

LEFT:
Two Girls at the Piano
c. 1890, oil on canvas, 44×34 inches (112.8×86.4 cm)
Metropolitan Museum of Art, New York
Robert Lehman Collection, 1975

ABOVE:
Girls Putting Flowers on Their Hats
1893-94, oil on canvas, 25½×20½ inches (65×52 cm)
E G Bührle Collection, Zurich

Woman with a Letter
1894, oil on canvas, 25½×21¼ inches (65×54 cm)
Musée de l'Orangerie, Paris

Gabrielle and Jean
c. 1895, oil on canvas, 25½×21½ inches (65×54 cm)
Musée de l'Orangerie, Paris

LEFT:
Misia Sert
1904, oil on canvas, 36×23½ inches (91.4×58.4 cm)
National Gallery, London

ABOVE:
Strawberries
c. 1905, oil on canvas, 11×18⅛ inches (28×46 cm)
Musée de l'Orangerie, Paris

ABOVE:
Claude Renoir Playing
c. 1905, oil on canvas, 18⅛×22 inches (46×55 cm)
Musée de l'Orangerie, Paris

RIGHT:
The Toilet: Woman Combing her Hair
1907-08, oil on canvas, 22×18¼ inches (55×46.5 cm)
Musée d'Orsay, Paris

PAGE 114:
Portrait of Ambroise Vollard
1908, oil on canvas, 31⅛×25½ inches (79×65 cm)
Courtauld Institute Galleries, University of London

PAGE 115:
Claude Renoir as a Clown
1909, oil on canvas, 47¼×30⅓ inches (120×77 cm)
Musée de l'Orangerie, Paris

Dancing Girl with Tambourine
1909, oil on canvas
61×25½ inches (155×65 cm)
National Gallery, London

Dancing Girl with Castanets
1909, oil on canvas
61×25½ inches (155×65 cm)
National Gallery, London

Monsieur and Madame Bernheim de Villers
1910. oil on canvas, 31⅞×25¾ inches (81×65.5 cm)
Musée d'Orsay, Paris

Madame Renoir and Bob
c.1910, oil on canvas, 32×25⅝ inches (81×65 cm)
Wadsworth Atheneum, Hartford, Connecticut
Ella Gallup Sumner and Mary Catlin Sumner Collection

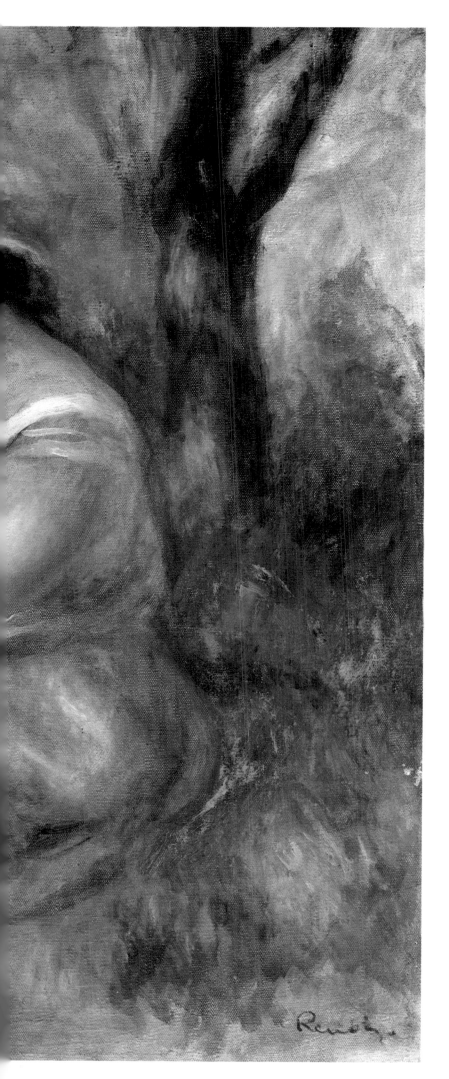

Seated Couple
1912, oil on canvas
20½×24¾ inches (52×63 cm)
National Museum of Wales, Cardiff

PAGE 122:
Gabrielle with a Rose
1911, oil on canvas
22¼×18½ inches (55.5×47 cm)
Musée d'Orsay, Paris

Page 123:
Tilla Durieux
1914, oil on canvas
36¼×29 inches (92×73.2 cm)
The Metropolitan Museum of Art,
New York
Bequest of Stephen C Clark, 1960

Judgment of Paris
1913-14, oil on canvas
28¼×36¼ inches (73×92 cm)
Hiroshima Museum of Art

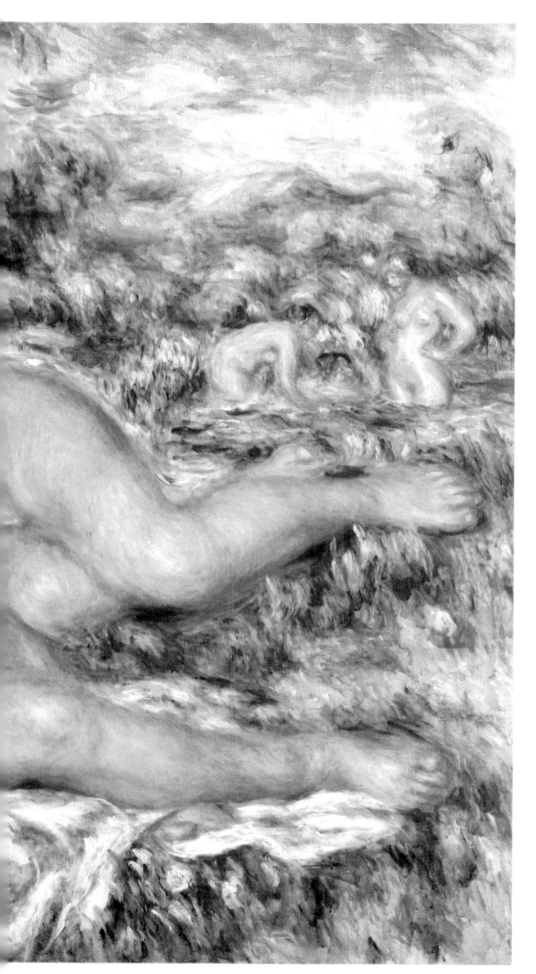

The Bathers
1918-19, oil on canvas
43⅓×63 inches (110×160 cm)
Musée d'Orsay, Paris

Acknowledgments

The publisher would like to thank Mike and Sue Rose of Casebourne Rose, Brighton, who designed this book. We would also like to thank the following institutions, agencies and individuals for supplying the illustrations:

Aberdeen Art Gallery: pages 98-99

The Art Institute of Chicago: pages 70-71 (Potter Palmer Collection), 73 (Potter Palmer Collection), 77 (Mr and Mrs Lewis Larned Coburn Collection), 86 (Mr and Mrs Martin A Ryerson Collection)

BPL: pages 8 (below), 11 (above)

Cleveland Museum of Art: page 105 (Bequest of Leonard C Hanna Jr)

Courtauld Institute Galleries, University of London: pages 51, 114

E G Bührle Collection, Zurich: pages 78, 107

Fine Arts Museum of San Francisco: page 39 (Gift of Mr and Mrs Prentice Cobb Hale in honor of Thomas Carr Howe Jr)

Fitzwilliam Museum, Cambridge: page 79

Fogg Art Museum, Harvard University, Cambridge, Massachusetts: page 17 (Grenville L Winthrop Bequest)

Folkwang Museum, Essen: page 24

Hiroshima Museum of Art: pages 124-125

Kröller-Müller Museum, Otterlo: page 27

Kunsthalle, Hamburg: page 48

Metropolitan Museum of Art, New York: pages 68-69 (Wolfe Fund, 1907, Catharine Lorillard Wolfe Collection), 88 (Bequest of Mrs H O Havemeyer, The H O Havemeyer Collection, 1929), 106 (Robert Lehman Collection, 1975), 123 (Bequest of Stephen C Clark, 1960)

The Minneapolis Institute of Arts: pages 84-85 (John R Van Derlip Fund)

Musée du Louvre/Réunion des Musées Nationaux: pages 6, 7 (above), 13

Musée Marmottan, Paris: page 45

Musée de l'Orangerie, Paris: pages 40, 60-61 (Collection Walter et Guillaume), 108, 109, 111, 112, 115

Musée d'Orsay, Paris/Réunion des Musées Nationaux: pages 7 (below), 8 (above), 16, 20, 56, 63, 64-65, 66-67, 83, 89, 91, 92, 113, 118, 122, 126-127

Musée du Petit Palais, Paris: page 14

Museu de Arte de São Paulo: pages 19, 38, 82, 103

Museum of Fine Arts, Boston: pages 35 (Bequest of John T Spaulding), 87 (Julia Cheney Edwards Collection), 90 (Picture Fund Purchase)

Museum of Fine Arts, Houston: page 41

National Gallery, Berlin: pages 25, 96-97

National Gallery, London: pages 4, 10, 28-29, 72, 74-75, 94-95, 102, 110, 116, 117

National Gallery of Art, Washington DC: pages 21 (Chester Dale Collection), 36-37 (Chester Dale Collection), pages 42-43 (Ailsa Mellon Bruce Collection), 50 (Widener Collection), 54-55 (Ailsa Mellon Bruce Collection)

Nationalmuseum, Stockholm: pages 18, 30-31

National Museum of Wales, Cardiff: pages 49, 120-121

National Museum of Western Art, Tokyo: page 44 (Matsukata Collection)

Norton Simon Art Foundation, Pasadena, California: pages 22-23

Oskar Reinhart Collection 'am Römerholz', Winterthur: pages 32-33, 57

Philadelphia Museum of Art: pages 58 (The Henry P McIlhenny Collection in memory of Frances P McIlhenny), 93, 100-101 (Mr and Mrs Carroll S Tyson Collection)

The Phillips Collection, Washington DC: pages 80-81

Portland Art Museum, Portland, Oregon: pages 52-53

Saint Louis Art Museum, St Louis, Missouri: Museum Purchase: page 34

Collection Sirot/Weidenfeld Archive: page 9

Staatsgalerie, Stuttgart: pages 1, 62

Städelsches Kunstinstitut, Frankfurt: pages 2, 76

Wadsworth Atheneum, Hartford, Connecticut: pages 46-47 (Bequest of Anne Parish Titzell), 119 (Ella Gallup Sumner and Mary Catlin Sumner Collection)

Wallraf-Richartz-Museum, Berlin: page 26

Weidenfeld Archive: pages 11 (below), 12

Worcester Art Museum, Worcester, Massachusetts: page 59

Yale University Art Gallery, New Haven, Connecticut: page 104 (The Katharine Ordway Collection)